ROC
Records

By Jan M. Mike

CELEBRATION PRESS
Pearson Learning Group

The following people from **Pearson Learning Group**
have contributed to the development of this product:

Joan Mazzeo **Design**	**Editorial** Leslie Feierstone-Barna, Cindy Kane
Christine Fleming **Marketing**	**Publishing Operations** Jennifer Van Der Heide

Production Laura Benford-Sullivan
Content Area Consultant Amy Keller

The following people from **DK** have
contributed to the development of this product:

Art Director Rachael Foster

Martin Wilson **Managing Art Editor**	**Managing Editor** Marie Greenwood
Rebecca Johns **Design**	**Editorial** Patricia Moss, Selina Wood
Alison Prior **Picture Research**	**Production** Gordana Simakovic
Richard Czapnik, Andy Smith **Cover Design**	**DTP** David McDonald

Consultant Keith Lye

Dorling Kindersley would like to thank Chanele Dandridge and Alastair Muir; Rose Horridge, Hayley Smith, and Gemma Woodward in the DK Picture Library; Johnny Pau for additional cover design work.

Photographs: Every effort has been made to secure permission and provide appropriate credit for photographic material. The publisher deeply regrets any omission and pledges to correct errors called to its attention in subsequent editions.

Unless otherwise acknowledged, all photographs are the property of Dorling Kindersley.

Photo locators denoted as follows: Top (T), Center (C), Bottom (B), Left (L), Right (R), Background (Bkgd)

Picture Credits: CVRBL Ryan Mathieu/Alamy; **BCVR** Oksana Perkins/Fotolia; **001** Simonkr/Fotolia; **003B** Linda Burgess/DK Images; **004B** Oksana Perkins/Fotolia; **005TR** KUCO/Shutterstock; **006B** Dr. Robert F. Dill/NOAA, **006T** Boyan Dimitrov/Fotolia; **007BR** Adam Sylvester/Science Source; **012TL** Stocktrek/Brand X Pictures/Getty Images; **013BL** Rainer Albiez/Fotolia; **014TL** NASA; **016B** Skyesnaps/Fotolia; **017BL** Angela Köhler/Fotolia, **017CL** Afitz/Fotolia, **017CR** Jeffrey Daly/Fotolia; **018BL** Martin M303/Fotolia; **019R** Wilm Ihlenfeld/Fotolia, **019R** c/Fotolia, **019R** Grandaded/Fotolia, **019R** Neilrod/Fotolia, **019R** MG1408/Fotolia; **020BL** Bettmann/Corbis, **020CL** Colin Keates/DK Images; **021B** Reb/Fotolia; **022BR** Sinclair Stammers/Science Source, **022BL** Sinclair Stammers/Science Source, **022TR** Scenics & Science/Alamy; **023CR** Colin Keates/Courtesy of the Natural History Museum, London/DK Images; **024BL** Giuliano Fornari/DK Images, **024TR** Sedgwick/DK Images; **026BR** Dr. Kari Lounatmaa/Science Source, **026TR** Harry Taylor/Courtesy of the Hunterian Museum (University of Glasgow)/DK Images; **027B** Colin Keates/Courtesy of the Natural History Museum, London/DK Images; **028B** Mat Hayward/Fotolia; **029TR** James King-Holmes/Science Source; **030B** Monty Rakusen/Cultura/Getty Images; **031BL** Sophie Warny and Kate Griener (Louisiana State University, Baton Rouge)/NASA, **031TR** Lora Koenig and Jessica Williams/NASA; **034BR** Rafael Ben-Ari/Fotolia; **035CRA** Andy Crawford/DK Images; **036B** Peter Marble/Fotolia, **036T** Dave King/Courtesy of the National Museum of Wales/DK Images; **037BL** Walter Mooney/U.S. Geological Survey.

All other images: DK Dorling Kindersley © 2005. For further information see www.dkimages.com

ISBN: 0-7652-5264-3

Color reproduction by Colourscan, Singapore
Printed in the United States of America
7 8 9 10 11   V0SV   17 16 15 14 13

1-800-321-3106
www.pearsonlearning.com

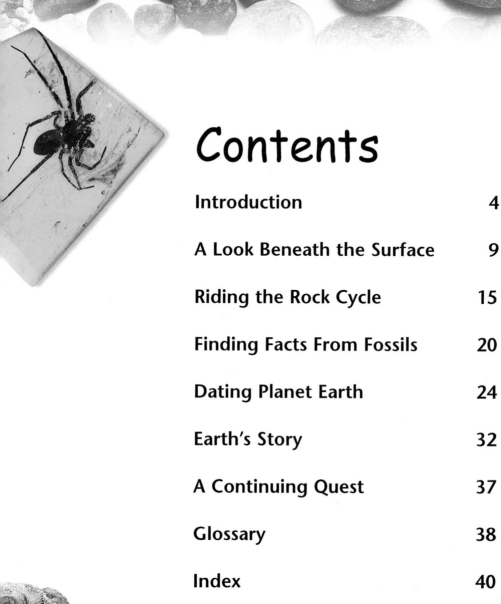

Contents

Introduction

Humans have asked questions about the land around them for thousands of years. What is Earth made of? What makes the ground quake and volcanoes erupt? How can there be seashells on mountain peaks? Over the years, we have made many discoveries about our planet by studying rocks.

There are many practical reasons to find out about Earth. Humans have long used rocks and minerals—from the simplest stone tools to metals used to build intricate machinery—to make life easier. In addition, by learning about the processes that shape our planet, scientists can try to prevent loss of life and property caused by earthquakes and volcanoes.

early stone ax
with a flint head

Humans are curious, too. As we study the evidence of past events in rocks—the rock record—we discover clues about Earth's history. We can begin to understand how our planet and the life it supports have changed over time.

Sedimentary rock is deposited in layers.

The Paria Wilderness Area in Arizona, United States, is made up of sedimentary rock that has been laid down over millions of years.

Spinning Tales

For thousands of years, people invented myths and legends to explain what they could not otherwise understand. When the ancient Greeks dug up fossils of mammoths and dinosaurs that no longer existed, they must have wondered where such strange creatures came from. Some researchers theorize that Greek tales about giants who once walked the Earth and battled against the gods might have been spun to explain the fossils people discovered.

The fictional Greek character, Odysseus, is fighting a Cyclops.

One such fossil is of *Deinotherium giganteum*, an animal related to the elephant. The skull, found on the Greek island of Crete, has a large opening in the center. This might have inspired tales of the one-eyed giant, the Cyclops.

Many such legends exist around the world. It was not until the Renaissance that people began to use more scientific approaches to try to answer their questions. The scientific method of questioning, observing, and experimenting has provided real insights into the history of our planet.

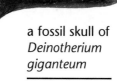

long tusks

a fossil skull of *Deinotherium giganteum*

5

What Is Geology?

Geology is the science that seeks to understand our planet through its rocks. Geologists study all parts of Earth, from huge jagged mountains to tiny grains of sand. They drill for samples of rock far below the planet's surface. They gather specimens from the highest peaks. They also investigate the bottom of the ocean floor.

Trans Hex diamond mine in South Africa contains a reddish soil that is full of diamonds.

Although it seems as if Earth is constant and unchanging, nothing could be further from the truth. The planet Earth is always changing. Some changes, such as a powerful earthquake, can be felt. Other changes can only be detected by sensitive scientific instruments. Some changes are quick and spectacular, such as the hot fury of a volcanic eruption. Others, such as the slow growth of a mountain range, take far longer than a human life span.

Geologists study mounds called stromatolites on the seabed. They are formed by algae and some are as old as 3.5 billion years.

Many Types of Geology

Geology is divided into many fields of study. Most geologists specialize in a particular area. Focusing closely on one area of study allows geologists to gain detailed knowledge.

Petrologists study rocks—what they are made of and where they came from. Seismologists study earthquakes. They look for clues to what goes on below the surface before earthquakes happen. They also measure an earthquake's power and intensity.

Although most people would try to avoid the fiery eruption of a volcano, volcanologists try to get close to a volcano to study it. They want to know what volcanoes can reveal about how Earth was formed and how it moves today. Historical geologists study how Earth has changed since it formed more than 4.6 billion years ago. Paleontologists focus on the history of life on Earth. They use clues found in rocks to learn about animals that lived long ago.

Volcanologists take samples of molten lava from volcanoes to learn what happens deep inside Earth.

This fossil is an example of the remains of a creature that once lived in the sea.

Tools of the Trade

For years, geologists used microscopes and chemicals as well as picks, mallets, hammers, and other tools to study rocks. Recent technology has become an important part of the geologist's equipment. Advanced measuring devices, computers, and tools that measure the motion of atoms record and process data that humans could not observe otherwise.

Using these modern tools and scientific techniques, geologists continue to uncover the rich history of our ever-changing planet.

Geologists use trowels and brushes to clear soil away from rocks. They sieve the soil for small particles of fossils and rock.

High-Tech Tools

Technology has given scientists new ways to examine rock samples and geological processes.

Seismographs measure shock waves in Earth by changing motion into electrical impulses. Then they measure and graph the shock waves.

Acceleration mass spectrometers measure how quickly certain atomic particles decay. They are useful for measuring the age of an object.

Electron microscopes use electrons instead of light waves to "illuminate" an object for closer study. Because electron waves are smaller than visible light waves, they can provide finer detail than a regular microscope can.

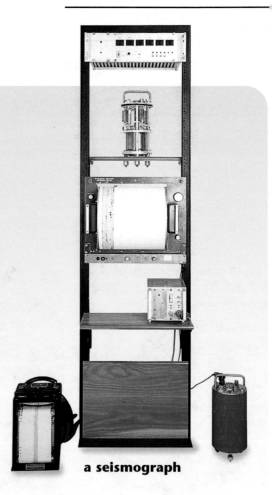

a seismograph

Geologists can take samples from only a short distance beneath Earth's surface. To theorize about what is farther down in Earth, geologists use their knowledge about what happens in the top layer, the **crust**. They also use what they know about minerals and their properties.

At the center of our planet is a hot, dense **inner core** of iron. It reaches temperatures usually estimated at 5,500 degrees to 9,000 degrees Fahrenheit. The inner core is hot enough to melt. However, the pressure of the rest of Earth on the core keeps it solid. A liquid **outer core** surrounds this mainly iron center.

The layer above the inner and outer cores is called the **mantle**. The mantle forms almost 80 percent of the total volume of Earth. Though the mantle is mostly solid, the top is partly molten and composed of superheated liquid rock called magma. Above the mantle, the crust ranges in depth from 3 to 40 miles.

This cutaway illustration shows the layers beneath the surface of Earth.

atmosphere

crust

mantle

outer core

inner core

The Lithosphere and Tectonic Plates

Scientists use two different concepts when they discuss Earth's outer part. They refer to the physical make-up of the layers—the crust and mantle. They also consider the movement of those layers.

Together, the crust and the rocky outer part of the mantle can move around on Earth's surface. These layers of crust and outer mantle, are called the **lithosphere**. The lithosphere covers the entire Earth, though it is broken up into **tectonic plates**—large sheets of thick rock. The partly fluid rock layer underneath the lithosphere, on which the plates move, is called the **asthenosphere**.

There are two types of tectonic plates: continental and oceanic. The continents of Earth are deeply embedded into continental plates. Oceanic plates lie beneath the seafloor.

Geologists have mapped out the plates that make up the lithosphere.

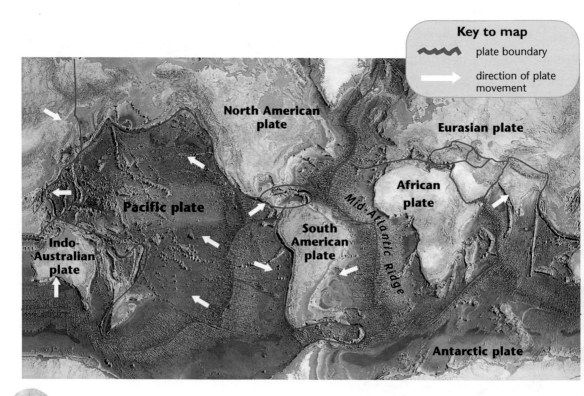

Key to map

〜〜〜 plate boundary

→ direction of plate movement

North American plate

Eurasian plate

African plate

Pacific plate

Mid-Atlantic Ridge

Indo-Australian plate

South American plate

Antarctic plate

The study of these continental and oceanic plates is called plate tectonics. Seven large plates and many smaller ones float on the molten rock of the mantle. The hot, thick liquid slowly churns, so the plates are in constant motion. This movement of tectonic plates is one of the forces that has shaped our Earth.

Continental Drift

Early in the twentieth century, Alfred Wegener, a German meteorologist, gathered evidence that supported the theory of continental drift. This theory says that continents change position on Earth's surface as the plates on which they rest move.

According to this theory, more than 200 million years ago, all the continents on our planet may have been part of one huge landmass, called Pangaea (pan-JEE-uh). As time passed, the movement of tectonic plates gradually pulled this supercontinent apart. Pangaea split into smaller pieces. The pieces eventually drifted apart and formed our modern continents.

The theory did not gain much support until the 1950s and 1960s. Scientists were convinced after they saw evidence of tectonic plates on the ocean floor. The theories of plate tectonics and continental drift revolutionized geology.

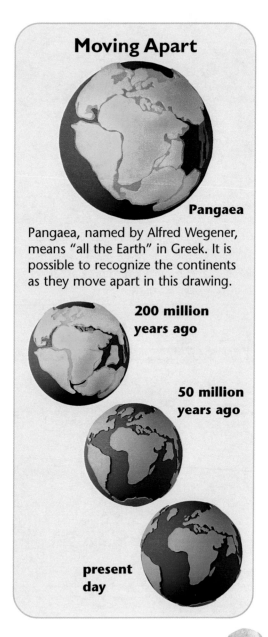

Moving Apart

Pangaea

Pangaea, named by Alfred Wegener, means "all the Earth" in Greek. It is possible to recognize the continents as they move apart in this drawing.

200 million years ago

50 million years ago

present day

The Shaking Earth

Tectonic plates slide against each other, push against each other, or pull away from each other at the edges where they meet. These movements crack and fold Earth's crust near the edge of the plates. A break in the crust along which plates move is called a fault. A plate edge can be as small as a wrinkle or as wide as a mountain.

Earthquakes occur along faults. Many quakes are so slight that people do not notice them. However, seismographs can measure these plate movements. Plates may also slide very rapidly, or even become stuck. Tremendous force builds as they push past each other, until rock along the fault slips, sending out vibrations called seismic waves. These seismic waves signal that an earthquake has occurred.

The San Andreas fault line in California, United States, has been created by the Pacific Ocean plate grinding past the North American plate.

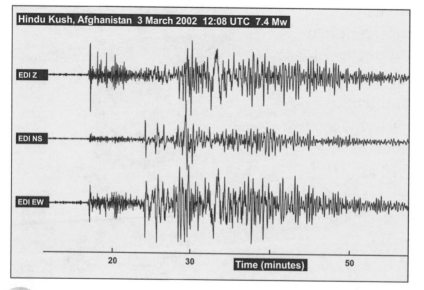

Hindu Kush, Afghanistan 3 March 2002 12:08 UTC 7.4 Mw

EDI Z

EDI NS

EDI EW

20   30   Time (minutes)   50

Earthquakes are measured according to the Richter scale, which measures the energy released in an earthquake.

The movement of tectonic plates is also responsible for the formation of mountains. Mountains can form in several different ways.

Volcanic Mountains

Volcanic mountains form mainly at the edges of tectonic plates, but they can also form over hot spots caused by plumes of magma deep within the mantle. The volcanoes of the Hawaiian Islands were formed when a plate passed over such a hot spot. The magma (molten rock) makes its way toward the surface of Earth's crust and forms the volcano.

Magma contains carbon dioxide gas—the same gas that makes carbonated beverages bubbly. The more carbon dioxide gas and dissolved water vapor that magma has, the more likely the magma is to erupt. It forces its way up through solid rock and pours out through an opening called a vent.

Magma erupting from Earth creates volcanic mountains.

Some Common Volcano Types

stratovolcano

Stratovolcanoes, also called composite volcanoes, are often cone-shaped. Most stratovolcanoes are formed by repeated explosive eruptions of magma.

shield volcano

Shield volcanoes are called that because they are thought to look like a broad, sloped warrior's shield. They are formed when lava flows for miles without cooling.

caldera volcano

Caldera volcanoes have a large, round, sunken area at the top. They form when magma erupts with enough force to collapse the ground underneath.

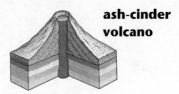

ash-cinder volcano

Cinder cones, also cone-shaped, have very steep sides. They are made from cinders of lava, or magma that has emerged from the volcano, and are often formed in one explosive eruption.

Fault-Block Mountains

Fault-block mountains are formed when two tectonic plates jostle against each other. Massive blocks of rock called horsts are gradually lifted between faults formed by plate movements. These horsts are called **fault-block mountains**. Tectonic plates can rub in three general directions: horizontal, vertical, and oblique (any sort of diagonal direction). This is the main reason fault-block mountains take different forms and shapes.

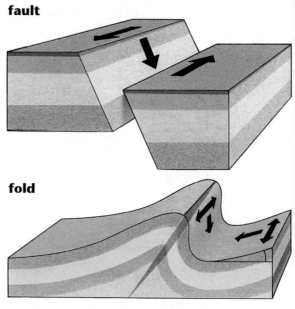

fault

fold

Faults and folds, both created by the movements of tectonic plates, form different types of mountains.

The Himalayas in south Asia were formed when a plate carrying India collided with the Eurasian plate.

Folded Mountains

Folded mountains form when one plate buckles and folds over another as they push against each other. Folded mountains can be as small as a hill or as large as a huge mountain range. The Himalayas, for example, are a folded mountain range that started to form when the continental plates of Asia and India began to collide about 50 million years ago.

Riding the Rock Cycle

Geologists study how rocks form. The **rock cycle** is the term used to describe how old rocks transform into new ones. This process has gone on since Earth formed. There are three major categories of rock: **igneous** (IG-nee-uhs) **rock**, **sedimentary rock**, and **metamorphic rock**.

Weathering, chemical reactions, pressure, and heat are forces involved in the rock cycle. Weathering grinds rocks into smaller particles that can form new rock. Chemical reactions and pressure can change the mineral composition of rock. Heat can melt rock and reform it.

Igneous rock is weathered and eroded.

Volcano erupts lava and ash.

Ash and grains of rock form in layers.

The Rock Cycle

igneous rock

Some sedimentary and metamorphic rock wear away to form new layers.

Magma rises and erupts as lava.

Igneous rock forms when erupted lava cools.

Igneous rock forms when magma cools under ground.

Rock melts to form magma.

sedimentary rock

Heat and pressure recrystallize rock into other rock.

metamorphic rock

Rock may melt to make new magma.

igneous rock

pumice floating on water

The igneous rocks pumice (floating on water in the photograph) and obsidian have the same chemical composition. The differences in their appearance are mainly a result of the conditions in which they form.

obsidian, a natural glass

Igneous Rock

Granite and basalt are examples of igneous rocks. They are formed from magma in the heat of the mantle. Igneous rocks are the building blocks of Earth. Magma moves from the upper mantle and lower crust, then cools into igneous rock. Factors that geologists use to classify different types of igneous rocks include their color and texture, their mineral composition, and where they formed.

The Cuillin Hills in the Isle of Skye, Scotland, contain different igneous rocks, including gabbro, granite, and basalt.

Cooling Off

Magma that reaches the surface of Earth while still in a liquid form is exposed to a sudden change in temperature. It solidifies quickly. Igneous rocks that form this way are classified as extrusive.

When magma begins to cool before a volcanic eruption, it solidifies slowly. The extra time allows minerals to arrange themselves into crystal form. This process is known as crystallization. The longer it takes magma to solidify, the more time there is for crystals to form. These types of igneous rocks are classified as intrusive. Valuable minerals often form in cavities in intrusive igneous rock.

pyrite

gold in quartz

_____

Slow cooling allows the minerals in magma to form crystals.

amethyst

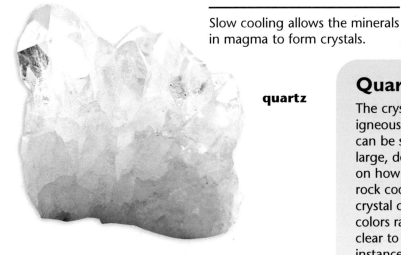
quartz

Quartz

The crystals in the igneous rock quartz can be small or large, depending on how quickly the rock cooled. Quartz crystal comes in colors ranging from clear to purple. For instance, amethyst is a quartz that is purple. The difference in color may be because of minerals or other impurities in the quartz, such as iron oxide.

emerald

Sedimentary Rock

Sedimentary rock is formed by deposits of natural materials. Geologists classify sedimentary rocks as clastic and non-clastic. The formation of clastic sedimentary rocks begins when weathering produces particles of rock and soil. Wind, water, or glaciers deposit these rocky bits to form **sediments**.

Over millions of years, layers of sediment are pressed together into rock. Conglomerate is one type of clastic rock. Formed by large particles, it looks like a handful of rounded pebbles glued together. Conglomerate forms on beaches or in rivers. Sandstone is another common sedimentary rock. It forms from small particles of sand. Shale and mudstone are made from the smallest particles, tiny grains of silt or clay.

Non-clastic sedimentary rocks can form from chemicals dissolved in rainwater. Rock salt and gypsum are examples. Other sedimentary rocks, such as most limestone, are biologics, and are made mainly from the remains of living things.

limestone

Sedimentary rocks may not look alike, but they are created by the same process.

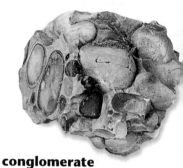

conglomerate

red sandstone

Composed primarily of sedimentary rock, including limestone and sandstone, the Grand Canyon in Arizona, United States, is an example of how weathering has shaped rocks.

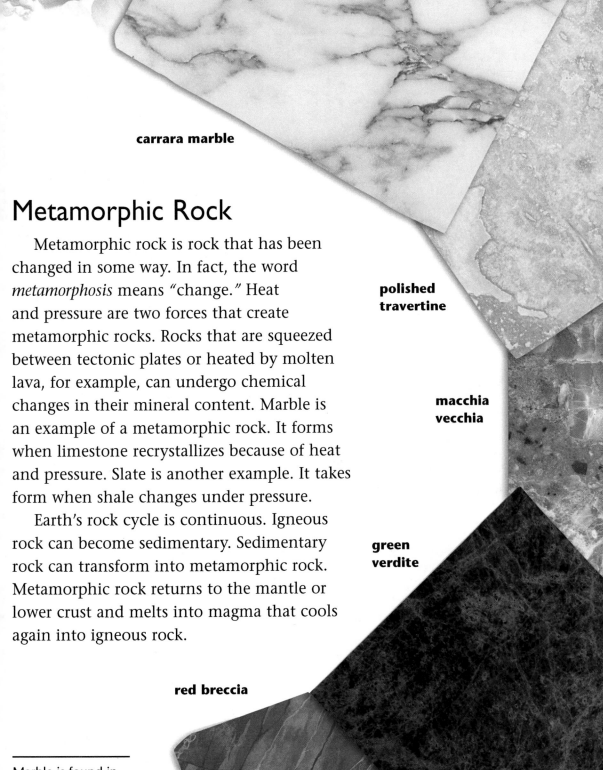

carrara marble

Metamorphic Rock

Metamorphic rock is rock that has been changed in some way. In fact, the word *metamorphosis* means "change." Heat and pressure are two forces that create metamorphic rocks. Rocks that are squeezed between tectonic plates or heated by molten lava, for example, can undergo chemical changes in their mineral content. Marble is an example of a metamorphic rock. It forms when limestone recrystallizes because of heat and pressure. Slate is another example. It takes form when shale changes under pressure.

Earth's rock cycle is continuous. Igneous rock can become sedimentary. Sedimentary rock can transform into metamorphic rock. Metamorphic rock returns to the mantle or lower crust and melts into magma that cools again into igneous rock.

polished
travertine

macchia
vecchia

green
verdite

red breccia

Marble is found in
a variety of different
colors and textures.

Finding Facts From Fossils

People have found and wondered about fossils for centuries. Fossils are the remains or other evidence (such as footprints or teeth marks) of once-living plants or animals preserved in rock. Fossils help us date rocks. They can also tell us about the history of life on Earth.

This fossilized trilobite cast shows how completely fossilization preserves the detail of creatures long dead.

This glossopteris fossil is an ancient fern leaf. Many fossils are found across the southern hemisphere in what was the supercontinent of Gondwanaland.

Trace Fossils

These are molds of footprints from two early humans made 3.6 million years ago in volcanic ash in Tanzania.

Many plants and animals left fossilized records of their existence, usually through impressions called trace fossils. Though the plant or animal may no longer exist, a replica forms within hardened sediment. Trace fossils include molds and casts. A mold forms when an impression hardens into rock, while a cast forms when a mold fills up with sediment and hardens. These can give us a detailed record of many kinds of organisms.

Permineralization

Harder materials can fossilize in a different way. Materials, such as wood, bone, and shell contain tiny holes. Minerals from water slowly fill the holes, and crystals begin to form inside. The original material keeps its shape. This process is called permineralization.

Sometimes the minerals replace most or all of the original material. This process, a type of permineralization, is called **petrifaction**, which means "change to stone." Petrified wood is an example of petrifaction. A piece of petrified wood feels as heavy as a rock, but still looks like wood.

Between 135 and 200 million years ago, this coral lived in a warm, shallow reef. Coral, like wood and bone, is frequently found permineralized.

The Petrified Forest National Park, Arizona, United States, contains the fossilized remains of 225-million-year-old trees.

The Tiniest Fossils

Microfossils, less than a twenty-fifth of an inch across, may be too small to see with the unaided eye. Like larger fossils, they are often found in rocks brought up from the depths of Earth by drilling.

Microorganisms, such as bacteria, are the oldest forms of life to leave a fossil record. Spores and pollen from the earliest plant life have been preserved as microfossils, although the plants they came from may not have fossilized. Scanning under an electron microscope can reveal the tiniest details of microfossils. Careful examination of such tiny fossils can give important information about what types of early life existed on Earth and how they evolved.

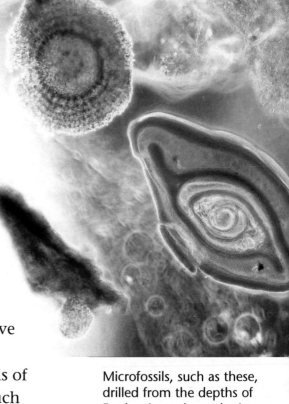

Microfossils, such as these, drilled from the depths of Earth, give paleontologists important information about early life on our planet.

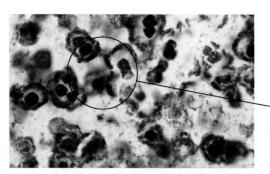

These 2-billion-year-old microfossils, found in Gunflint chertz rock in Ontario, Canada, are the earliest evidence of life found so far.

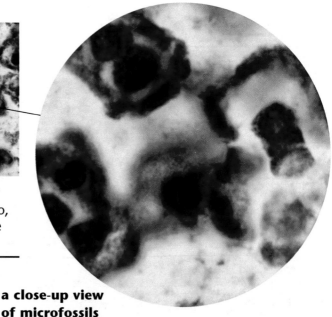

a close-up view of microfossils

Trapped in the resin of a prehistoric plant that hardened into amber, this spider still looks ready to take its next step after waiting millions of years.

Fixed in Time

Amber is fossilized plant sap, or resin. Tiny prehistoric creatures are sometimes preserved in amber. These creatures were trapped on the sticky surface of an ancient plant or tree, and then they were covered with even more resin. The resin hardened into amber, preserving the finest details of the trapped creatures. Delicate pseudoscorpions, mushroom flies, and other animals have left a record of their existence in this way.

This ancient maple seed has been perfectly preserved as a fossil.

Ancient plants also left records in a process called carbonization. Plants are preserved in fossil form when leaves and stems are quickly buried and flattened. As sediment layers form above the trapped plant, the pressure builds. The leaves and stem are squeezed into a thin carbon film, making a "fossil photograph" of a plant.

Coal is a very common form of carbonized prehistoric plant life, but undistorted fossils are rare.

Dating Planet Earth

It is possible to discover when life began and how Earth and the life it supports have changed over the years. Events on Earth have left clues. Geologists and paleontologists work together to learn as much as they can. As they decipher rock and fossil records, we gain an understanding of how life has developed and changed.

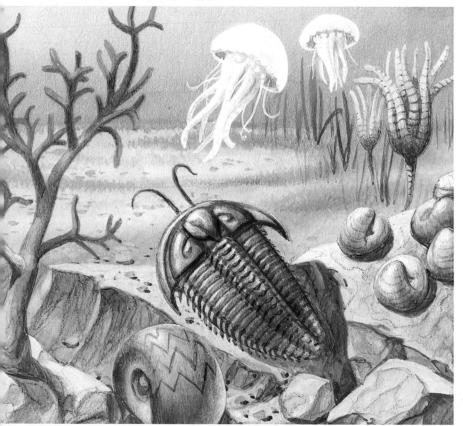

When fossils of extinct marine invertebrates, such as trilobites, are found on mountain peaks, scientists gain insight into how Earth has changed.

This artist's impression of life 500 million years ago may have been based on information from the Burgess Shale, an important fossil site in the Canadian Rockies.

Relative Dating

In nineteenth-century England, a man named William Smith came to an important realization. Smith, an engineer and a canal surveyor, realized that undisturbed layers of rock, or strata, carry a portrait of Earth's history. This realization became the core of an entire geological science called stratigraphy, or the study of strata. Smith made the first geological maps.

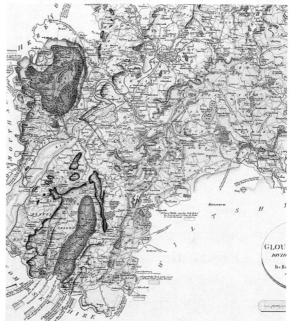

This section of a map, drawn by William Smith, indicates the geological ages he discovered represented in the strata of Gloucestershire in the United Kingdom.

When strata are undisturbed, the bottom layer of a rock bed is normally the oldest layer. Each successive layer of rock formed later, on top of the layer beneath. Understanding which layers were laid down when makes it possible to compare the age of fossils found in the rock bed. Any fossil found in a lower layer of rock would be older than fossils found in the upper strata. This form of dating rock layers and the fossils found in them is called **relative dating**.

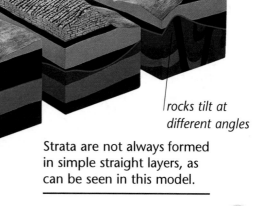

rocks tilt at different angles

disturbance in the layered sequence of rock

Strata are not always formed in simple straight layers, as can be seen in this model.

Index Fossils

Relative dating also provides a way to compare information from different locations. Rocks that contain the same species of fossils, even if they are in different types of rocks or far apart in the world, may well have developed during the same time.

Scientists have divided the ages of Earth into four main groups, or eras. The earliest is the **Precambrian era**, which started about 4,600 million years ago. Time from about 570 million years ago to the present is divided into three eras. The **Paleozoic era** lasted from about 570 to 250 million years ago. The **Mesozoic era** lasted from about 250 to 65 million years ago and the **Cenozoic era** started about 65 million years ago and is still continuing. Each of these three eras is divided into smaller time sections called periods.

Fossils of species found in several layers of rock strata can tell us about broad periods of time. Other fossils, called **index fossils**, give us information about the specific strata in which they are found. These fossils can help us estimate the age of a rock layer or the environment in which it was formed.

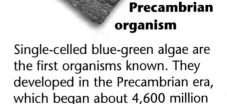

ediacara, Precambrian organism

Single-celled blue-green algae are the first organisms known. They developed in the Precambrian era, which began about 4,600 million years ago.

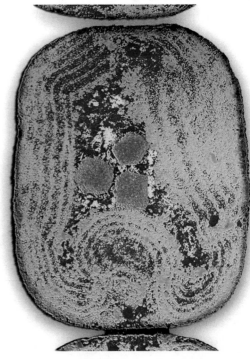

highly magnified image of blue-green algae, still living today

To be useful as an index fossil, a species must have evolved quickly and it must have become extinct in a short period. An index fossil must also come from an easily identified creature or plant whose remains are widely distributed in different locations. Various trilobites, shelled animals that once lived in the sea, are useful as index fossils. They are found only in rocks of the Paleozoic era.

Fossils provide scientists with a great deal of information. However, they usually cannot tell the exact age of a sedimentary layer. To establish an exact age, geologists use nearby igneous rocks.

trilobite, Paleozoic era

Trilobites thrived in the Paleozoic era. They flourished as swimmers, crawlers, and burrowers in shallow seas.

Ammonites were widespread in the Mesozoic era. These squid-like shellfish are only found in this era, making them important index fossils.

ammonite, Mesozoic era

giant cerith, Cenozoic era

Gastropods, such as snails, first appear in the fossil record during our current Cenozoic era.

Geological Rock Column

era	million years ago
Cenozoic era	
	65
Mesozoic era	
	250
Paleozoic era	
	570
Precambrian time	
	4,600

This geological rock column shows the four main eras into which Earth history is divided.

Radiometric Dating

Assigning an age in actual years is called **absolute dating**. This process was not possible until the discovery of radioactivity in the late nineteenth century. Radioactivity is the decay of the nucleus in the atoms of certain elements.

Dating objects by their radioactive decay is called radiometric dating. This process can date even the oldest rocks on Earth if they contain traces of radioactive elements, such as uranium or thorium. The breaking down of elements happens in a predictable process that can be measured. Scientists measure the decay in units called half-life. By comparing different types of elements in a certain rock, geologists can estimate how long the decay has been going on. This tells them the age of the rock.

A radiometric dating process called **radiocarbon dating** can be used to date more recent rocks and materials—less than 70,000 years old. Two forms of carbon are present in a certain ratio in all living things. When an organism dies, one form of carbon decays in a predictable way into nitrogen. By comparing the ratio of each form of carbon in a sample, it is possible to measure the sample's age.

Radiometric dating can be complicated and is not always accurate. For example, the radioactive elements in sedimentary rocks that are made up of weathered igneous rocks would tell when the original igneous rocks were formed. They wouldn't tell us when the sedimentary rock was laid down. Contamination by substances, such as groundwater, which may add carbon of a different age, can also cause errors. Whenever possible, more than one dating process is used.

Samples need to be carefully cleaned in a laboratory before they can be radiocarbon dated.

Radiocarbon dating on charcoal determined a volcano erupted 6,640 years ago to create Crater Lake in Oregon.

Using Absolute and Relative Dating

A set of rock layers containing a unique group of fossils is called a zone. When geologists study the fossil record in a particular zone, they can determine which creatures lived and died during a certain period. By using radiometric dating on igneous rocks in the same zone, geologists can determine the absolute age of the surrounding rocks. Using absolute and relative dating in fossil zones around the world has helped geologists construct a more accurate picture of Earth's history.

Igneous and sedimentary rocks in the same strata can be used to date index fossils.

Scientists use a mass spectrometer to determine the age of a sample through radiocarbon dating.

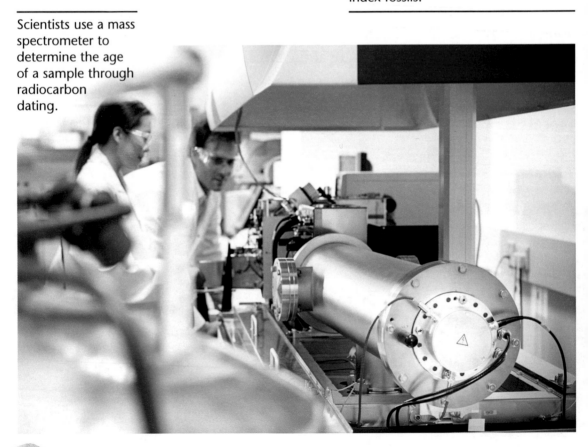

Other Dating Methods

New techniques are being developed to gather geological information. Using different methods can confirm dates and help scientists obtain a clear picture of how Earth and life on it has changed. The layers of silt, sand, and clay deposited by glaciers are examined to determine the composition of rocks and the climate of an area over time. Tree rings and fossilized pollen are also studied to date fossil zones more accurately.

Geologists continue to seek new methods to classify and date the huge numbers of fossils. From them, we are getting a good picture of Earth's history, backed by solid scientific evidence found in the rock records.

This ancient pollen grain from Antarctica can be studied under a microscope to learn what life was like 15-20 million years ago.

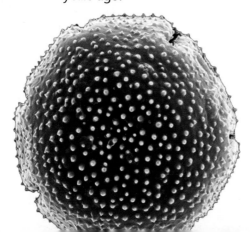

Scientists bore through the ice to take deep cylindrical cores. They study sections of the cores under powerful microscopes.

Earth's Story

Billions of years ago, as the newly formed Earth cooled into a ball of rock and metal, huge volcanic eruptions spewed ash and gases into the air. Clouds formed from the floating ash, shading Earth from the direct heat of the Sun.

Chemical changes took place as the planet cooled. Oceans formed and an atmosphere grew. The young Earth was a world of violent lightning storms and volcanic eruptions. It was a vastly different place than the home we know. All of these physical and chemical forces combined and reacted over many millions of years.

Small mammals appeared.

Dinosaurs became extinct.

Global mountain building occurred.

Soft-bodied animals appeared (e.g., worms and jellyfish).

Trilobites appeared.

PRECAMBRIAN

PALEOZOIC ERA

Organisms appeared (e.g., blue-green algae).

Earth formed.

Coral reefs appeared.

Marine plants flourished.

Land plants appeared.

Vertebrates appeared.

More complex types of algae appeared.

Geological time

This geological time scale shows the ages of Earth and when different life-forms appeared.

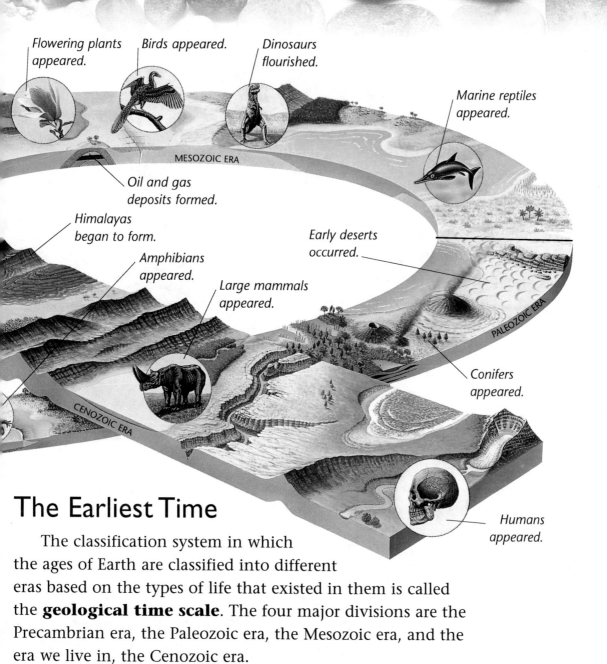

Flowering plants appeared.

Birds appeared.

Dinosaurs flourished.

Marine reptiles appeared.

MESOZOIC ERA

Oil and gas deposits formed.

Himalayas began to form.

Early deserts occurred.

Amphibians appeared.

Large mammals appeared.

PALEOZOIC ERA

Conifers appeared.

CENOZOIC ERA

Humans appeared.

The Earliest Time

The classification system in which the ages of Earth are classified into different eras based on the types of life that existed in them is called the **geological time scale**. The four major divisions are the Precambrian era, the Paleozoic era, the Mesozoic era, and the era we live in, the Cenozoic era.

The Precambrian era is the earliest era, and its life is the least well known because little record exists. During this time, life-forms evolved, or changed over time, from organisms with a single cell to more complex, multicelled plants and animals. Such soft organisms left few clues behind to tell their story, although some fossils have been found.

Life Blooms: The Paleozoic Era

The Paleozoic era began 570 million years ago and ended about 250 million years ago. During the Paleozoic era, life increased dramatically on Earth. Life evolved from more primitive organisms into animals, such as trilobites, sharks, and cockroaches. This development happened slowly, in stages.

Fossil records show that vast seas covered much of ancient Earth at times. Plant life evolved first in the oceans, along with many animal species. The seas receded and rose, again and again. Plants began to grow on Earth's surface. These plants eventually evolved into huge forests. When Earth had an atmosphere that could support animal life, the first amphibians left the water to live on land, at least some of the time.

Fish with jaws first developed in the Paleozoic era.

These giant tree ferns in New Zealand's Otari reserve are very similar to the landscape in the Paleozoic era.

The Age of Dinosaurs: The Mesozoic Era

The Mesozoic era started about 250 million years ago and ended about 65 million years ago. This is the period when dinosaurs evolved. These fascinating creatures ruled Earth for more than 150 million years. Clues in the fossil record help us understand how they lived.

During the Mesozoic era, the first birds took flight, and the earliest mammals evolved. These early mammals were small, and had little chance of competing with dinosaurs. However, at the end of the Mesozoic era, dinosaurs vanished and mammals thrived.

It's possible that a disaster, perhaps a meteor strike, had something to do with the disappearance of the dinosaurs. Rock records support this theory. A thin layer of clay has been found in rocks formed at the end of the Mesozoic era, 65 million years ago. This clay is rich in iridium—an element that is not usually found on Earth's surface, but is plentiful in meteorites.

The clay layers might have formed after an enormous meteorite slammed into Earth. Dust from the impact might have dimmed the sunlight, changing the climate of Earth and killing the plants that dinosaurs ate.

allosaurus skull

Fossilized skeletal remains, such as this skull, give geologists the information they need to reconstruct how dinosaurs probably looked.

reconstruction of an allosaurus

Glaciers and Mammals: The Cenozoic Era

The Cenozoic era is the time of mammals: animals that have hair, feed their young with milk, and are warmblooded. Mammals have large brains compared to other animals of comparable size. They learn well, perhaps because the young are fed and cared for by their parents. The fossil record in this era shows the development of familiar mammals of today and the rise of *Homo sapiens*, or human beings.

Glaciers, huge, thick sheets of ice, spread over Earth during part of the Cenozoic era. Many times glacial ice crumbled mountains and scraped Earth, then melted and retreated into mountain valleys. This is the period to which our earliest ancestors can be traced. As glaciers bridged the continents and sea levels changed, humans migrated across Earth. By testing human artifacts using radiocarbon dating, the timing of these migrations, and of the activity of the glaciers, can be discovered.

As glaciers covered Earth, animals were occasionally trapped in swampy areas and frozen. Ice preserved this mammoth for at least 12,000 years.

The giant Moai statues on Easter Island in the Pacific Ocean were carved out of volcanic rock by people 1,200 years ago.

A Continuing Quest

Although geologists and other scientists who study Earth have answered many questions about our planet, more questions always arise. Scientists continue to work together—and debate each other—to understand the processes that shape our planet. If you watch the world around you, you can see some of these processes at work. Whether it's a volcano blowing its top, a sandstorm weathering rock, an earthquake shaking a city, or just a simple stream smoothing its bed, you can see with your own eyes the processes that have shaped Earth for billions of years.

Geologists are constantly studying movements in Earth to anticipate and prepare for natural disasters, such as earthquakes.

Are You Interested in Geology?

Amateur geologists and paleontologists have made many important finds. The best way to get started with rock and fossil hunting is to contact collectors who are familiar with an area. They will be able to suggest tools and recommend sites where the best specimens might be found.

Safety equipment is important. Sturdy shoes, a hard hat, goggles, and gloves will provide protection. Carry a first-aid kit, maps, and a compass, and always go with an adult who knows the area. Be sure to take a camera to record discoveries made while you study our fascinating planet.

Glossary

absolute dating   the assignment of a specific age to a rock, fossil, or other object

asthenosphere   a partly molten layer near the edge of Earth's mantle, below the lithosphere

Cenozoic era   the most recent of the four major classifications of geologic time, including the present, when mammals evolved into a rich variety of species.

crust   the thin outer layer of Earth's surface

fault-block mountains   structures created by movements along faults

folded mountains   uplifts of varying sizes created by one tectonic plate buckling under another

geological time scale   the scale used to categorize geological formations by the age when they formed

igneous rock   rock formed from cooled magma

index fossils   fossils from a species known to have existed during a particular span of geologic time

inner core   the dense, primarily iron, center of Earth

lithosphere   the outer layer of Earth, made up of the crust and the outer part of the mantle

mantle   the semisolid rock layer between Earth's outer core and its crust, comprising almost 80 percent of the total volume of the planet

Mesozoic era   the third oldest of the four major classifications of geologic time, when dinosaurs dominated Earth

metamorphic rock   rock that is formed by changes caused by heat, contact, pressure, or other chemical changes

outer core

a liquid layer made up mostly of molten iron surrounding Earth's dense inner core

Paleozoic era

the second oldest of the four major divisions of geologic time, a time of expansion and evolution of many life-forms

petrifaction

process by which minerals replace organic material, and the material hardens into rock

Precambrian era

the oldest of the four major classifications of geologic time, when the planet formed and underwent severe environmental and chemical changes, and simple life-forms came into existence

radiocarbon dating

a form of absolute dating that measures the amount of undecayed carbon in an object to determine its age

relative dating

the assignment of an age to a rock or fossil in comparison to other rocks or fossils

rock cycle

the continuous transformation of old rocks into new ones by heat, pressure, weathering, and chemical reactions

sedimentary rock

rock that forms as sediment compresses or accumulates by chemical action over time

sediments

particles of rock deposited by wind, water, or glaciers

seismographs

machines used to measure the location and intensity of earthquakes

tectonic plates

large sections of the Earth's lithosphere that move

Index